BLACK BOOK OF POEMS
PART II

Also by Vincent K. Hunanyan

I Wasn't Crying Over You
Black Book of Poems

BLACK BOOK OF POEMS
PART II

Vincent K. Hunanyan

For You

PREFACE

On my twenty-sixth birthday I was in Vietnam, having a heart attack. It was also the day I published *Black Book of Poems*.

Having quit my sales job to heroically dedicate my life to this craft, I picked my birthday to be the release date for my first official work.

I had absolutely no expectations publishing *Black Book of Poems;* I knew the struggles of self-publishing and that a book (regardless of its quality) was never guaranteed sales. I told myself that if I could impact one reader out of a thousand, or even ten thousand, nothing else mattered.

I returned from the hospital at sunrise (my heart apparently healthy), published the book, and went to sleep. The rest, as they say, is history.

As I mentioned in my previous preface, there is no magic formula to understanding poetry. Poetry is not math—it's not perfect or precise. You don't "understand" it intellectually. I believe your connection with a good poem is more spiritual than anything.

Anyone forcing their interpretation of a poem on you is usually full of shit. Unless it's the author's will. But, then, what's the point in writing the piece in the first place?

The quality of a poem is not tied to the complexity of the words or the symmetry of the rhymes or meter. I think the best poems are simple but profound, free from sentiment yet somehow heartbreaking.

I have previously expressed my reluctance to explain my poetry and a while ago I found a quote by Tarkovsky that best justifies my sentiment: "A book read by a thousand different people is a thousand different books."

So don't fear poetry and don't overthink it. And if you don't "get it," don't force it. That's all. Come back to it and try again if you want.

All great art takes time to truly appreciate and resonate with. That's all there is to it.

Unlike the previous collection in which most poems have a rhyming scheme, the style within these pages will vary. As poetry can be very lyrical, for the best experience, read the poems out loud. It will also engage more of your senses.

P.S. My deepest gratitude to Patty Rice and the entire team at Andrews McMeel Publishing for doing a tremendous job. Thank you kindly.

ENJOY!

BLACK BOOK OF POEMS
PART II

THE STAGE (ACT II)

The music of division stops
Lights grow dark and bright
The orchestra starts from the top
In steps the Headless Knight

He carries something in his sack
The viewers cannot catch
Sir Walter Raleigh dressed in black
Steals it with a snatch

"I shall give you back your head
If you shall give me mine
Shortly, I must meet the dead
And want my mind to shine"

The head of state in blessing all
Prepares the children for the war
The Federal Reserve has warned
The world economy could fall!

The humble Sultan on his horse
Deciding, demonstrates remorse
Marco Polo drowns in sand
Never finding Neverland

She sings of death and Pepsi-Cola
The world is dying from ~~Ebola~~ corona
Last time the swine were causing flu
The papers claimed it to be true

Romeo enters, full of life
To an almost empty scene
Looking for his future wife
Who has scarcely turned thirteen

Which way is the Risin' Sun
Asks Bob Dylan on the run
Bukowski choking on a scotch
Is gladly pointing to his crotch

Her Majesty the Queen proclaims:
"Let them eat their tears!"
And looking to divert the blame
Resorts to force and fear

Promiscuity promoting proles
Change the sexes and their roles
The Communists behead the Tsar
For being in blood stepped in, too far

Balthasar onto the stage
Is entering in fright
Romeo looking at the page
Is trembling at the sight

"My gracious friend, your love is dead!"
Cries the loyal slave
"They have moved her from your bed
To the royal grave"

Shakespeare, passing, feebly yells:
"Do not touch my bones!
And to Hathaway do tell
She shall die alone!"

The final scene is drawing near
The lights grow bright and dark
The Tragic Hero drenched in fear
Is waiting for his mark

The curtains close; the stage is black
Behold! Here comes the final act.

IT, TOO, SHALL PASS

Every man must bear his cross,
Through pleasure, pain, and loss.
In empty fields of shallow graves,
Untainted souls will take my place.

And in your final, fading day,
Forget me not, my friend, I pray.
No pain can stay, no pleasures last;
Cry not, my love, it, too, shall pass.

PTSD (to be read in one breath)

Free World Leaders calmly selling
Trigger-happy soldiers, raping
Beaten children, hungry, crying
Broken veterans keep trying
Ravished villages collapsing
Orphaned children, hungry, dying
Propaganda keeps corrupting
The brightest minds of my generation
Feeble-minded freedom fighters
Public pressure, public panic
Hunting season is upon us

Now your arguments don't matter,
My opinions reign true.

EYES WIDE SHUT

I've seen the visions of the few
In dust and ashes on our knees
I've seen the barons shaking hands
In bitter, vigorous contempt

I've seen the parties promise peace
While sirens pierced my muted ears
I've seen my brother kill his blood
And lose his willingness to breathe

I've seen our children smile and nod
And swallow doctrines of the meek
I've seen it all with eyes wide shut
And prayed to pass it by, untouched.

FIX ME

Broken people try and fix me,
Blind men cry for me to see.

THE LONELY ONES

The gravedigger shall carry on
In distant, desolate rain
And years go by and they must learn
To love the growing pain

Until the drops of rain entwine
In soothing, solemn streaks
To wash anew their anguished hearts
And set their sorrows free.

A POEM

t
h
i
s

i
s

a

p
o
e
m

ANOTHER POEM

this

too

is

a

poem

SHE

I sang a song of desolate past
'Twas filled with angst and woe
An angel came before my eyes
In godly, golden glow

She smiled and stroked my worried mind
And cried for me to know
So I wept in great delight
For all the world to hear

She wiped and kissed my crimson cheeks
And whispered in my ear:
"If you believe, then so shall he
For whom you shed your tears."

ON IMPOVERISHED LIFE

Intruders ravished my garden
Beheading my plants
Ripping my trees
From their roots

Next, they planted a tree of their own
It grew very tall and mighty
No more sun my garden saw
And all my flowers winced away
The once green grass
Turned to
Dust,
And so

I ran,
And I ran,
And I ran.

IN BETWEEN

Here it goes:
You're the last person
I think of
before retiring to bed
and the first person
on my mind
as I awake

and in between
you've been my dreams.

TRIGGER WARNING

—LIFE

1984

Welcome to the Truman Show
Nineteen eighty-four
Go to bed, comrade, sleep tight
We will watch you in the night.

We will watch you in the day
You can stay—but not away
You can run but you can't hide
Until the day you lose your mind.

EX AND WHY

If you are born an X and Y,
Then predetermined shall you die.

RATS EAT ALL

The thief must steal his sister's meal
The righteous man must give
The soldier must *man up* and leave
The wretched mother—grieve

To the West all birds must fly
To the East the missiles drop
Ravished children live to die
Dogs eat corpses, rats eat all.

AS I LIE DYING IN MY SLEEP

As I lie dying in my sleep
The fairy, fiercely, flaps his wings
Old ladies cry in vain tonight
Many men with wounds found home

Pricking holes in broken skin
The shooter fires, sharp and still
The lights are on—let us dine in
The water's running for a while

In the mountains shots ring true
The earth beneath our feet is cracked
Swallowing our bliss
Thirty years perversely passed

Was it happiness we missed?

BENEATH THE EARTH

The storm is raging in the fields
And in the meadows bodies burn
Forsaken widows laugh in tears
The Savior, rueful, failed his turn

Beneath the earth their fathers lay
In time their sons will feed the worms
The firing squad shall shoot and miss
So they may cheat their destined day.

BREAKING NEWS

Turning on my smart TV
I killed my kin
R. E. L. U. C. T. A. N. T. L. Y.

MY ONE TRUE LOVE

My one true love is but a glimpse
Of blissful time, now long, long past
As such, I think what could have been
And whether we could truly last

We loved the only way we knew:
Relentlessly and impromptu
Lust was love and love was new
She has moved on, and I must, too.

SUFFERING

They say fine writing comes from suffering
—I must suffer more.

I THOUGHT

My priest once said
everything happens for a reason
and I thought of my Aunt
and her cancer
claiming her,
unforgivingly.

I thought of the bombs
falling over innocent people
living in remote villages
I couldn't pronounce
and of the mutilated corpses
of children
not older than myself.

Everywhere.

I even dared to think of *our* Genocide
and the forgotten souls, fading in history.

I thought and I thought,
and I was dazed for days and days.

NOT FAR

She makes me
Want to write again
Will this be sad,
I cannot say

She smells of home
A distant dream
I have foreseen
And now it's here

Her tongue is mine
Her eyes are mine
Will this be sad,
I think it might

Where will we go?
Not far I hope.

EVERYONE

Everyone's an activist
When the whistle's blown
Likeness in the symmetry
When the masks come on

No one looks under his nose
Until the stink's unbearable
Everybody looks about
When the bombs go off.

UNITED

Crowds unite and march in sync
Across the ocean corpses stink
The anger rages, loud and firm
Across the ocean cities burn

The masses gather round the tent
The boys in skirts are back
The flock is growing discontent
And paints the white house black.

REASON

It didn't take long until
I came to the bitter epiphany
that reason cannot soothe spiritual pain!

Frankly,
I did not anticipate the aftermath,
and the endless *what-ifs*
spinning in my head
on repeat
like a played-out song that makes you sick.

You see,
I never understood how people went
from intense intimacy to . . . strangers.

The funniest thing of all, though,
is how all these stupid
fucking heartbreak songs
all of a sudden make sense,
and I *really* don't like that.

You never miss your well . . .

Well, I think the water went sour
long before it dried out.

Hey!

Maybe one day, like a cliché,
we'll bump into each other in New York,
like we always said we would,
and I'll tell you I foolishly decided to
dedicate my life to this ungrateful passion,
and you'll tell me you're on Broadway,
and though we'll be truly happy for each other,
there will be a soft sadness in our eyes
as we could have shared this happiness.

Perhaps . . .

Anyway!

I wanted to write this down
so that one day I can look at this
and feel stupid;
more stupid than when I thought
reason could soothe emotional pain.

CONFINED

I am confined to my own mind
And can't escape these prison walls
For what I am is what I see
And what I see I'll always be.

WILL ANYONE DIE FOR MY SINS?

Will anyone die for my sins,
Or have I slept too long?
May Mother Mary birth a child
That I may drink his blood

To whom now shall I turn for help
When hope is all but gone?

At last,
Let's kill Him, once, for all,
And watch the West crumble and fall.

FREE

You don't   have to be   athletic
You don't   have to wear   cosmetics
You don't   have to make   him eggs
You don't   have to shave your legs
You don't   have to turn   the cheek
You don't   have to hear   him speak
You don't   have to trim   your pits
You don't   have to   mother kids
You can   rest assured   in glee!
      Now,
      will
      it really
      set
      you
      free?

LOVING IS A DYING ART

Loving is a dying art
And I am drained of love to give
Loving is a dying art
And all the poems meant for you
Felt forced
As I recited them
—For her

Loving is a dying art—
You ripped my ------- heart apart.

HELP ME, FATHER

Help me, Father, I am lost
All my heroes have sold out
Everything I thought I knew
Has proven false and true

Now I shall be the worst of them
And I will hate this world, forever
I shall spit upon its face
Now I will be the worst of them.

IN REMEMBRANCE OF LOST LOVE

The day you passed
I died with you
And everything
Once brave and true
Turned into dust.

The shine went out of everything
Your smile forever left in Spring
Your voice grows distant to my ears
Your smell is all I have of you
But even that is fading, too.

At night I lie awake in rue
I should've died instead of you.

FADING

Your beauty's fading every day
Your careless attitude persists
What of the day when all is lost
And no one's left to hold your hand

Inside the vacuum of your dreams
And all the shattered hopes of love.

YESTERDAY, MY LOATHING GREW

Yesterday, my loathing grew
Today, I'll blame my pain on you
Tomorrow, we shall all agree:
You must blame your pain on me.

ME

Do you still think of me,
as I still think of you?
Do you still dream of me,
as you're still in my dreams?

If so,
does the idea of me
widen your lips
or leave a bitter taste
upon your tongue?

WRITING IS A LONELY WORK

Writing is a hungry work
That feeds your inner beast
Only a fool devotes his life
To such ungrateful deeds.

YOU

With you,
my heart doesn't skip a beat—
It stops,
and in that lifeless glimpse of joy,
I see you.

I truly see *you*.

IN THE NAME OF FREEDOM

Kill us in the name of peace
And establish order
Who auctioned out and sold the lease?
Who's standing on the border?

Now all rise; salute the flag
In the name of freedom
Wheel in the veterans on ice
Make sure the children see them.

EVEN GOD

Even God must cry sometimes:
For beauty's sake, for pity's sake
For all the gentle hearts still beating
And all the noble acts of truth

For all the children left alone
And every soldier coming home
For all the families in pain
And all who give and keep on giving

For all the true, the brave and kind
Even God must cry sometimes.

FAIRY TALE

All fairy tales must reach their end
The hero triumph, good prevail
With the pretty maiden on his horse
Toward the sunset he must set

And happily forever after
They must live through thin and laughter!

FOREVER AFTER

Forever after seems so rare
Perhaps it's me—I'm getting old
The maidens give themselves away
Or maybe I'm just growing cold

What if the story's mine to write
Will I still wallow in my fears?

BABYSITTER

The babysitter has enslaved me;
I'm in a prison I can't see.
I'm in a place of endless laughter
and creeping, paralyzing fear.

Why should *I* care their homes are burning?
Our stars will always shine above.

> **"ANOTHER BOMB FELL;
> KIDS WERE LEARNING
> THE MEANING OF
> RESPECT AND LOVE."**

THE ONE

Who dares disturb me in the night?
    'Tis me, my Lord, your humble page
Step forth, at once, into the light;
Speak the message from the sage.

Thus spoke the servant with a leer:
    A storm will rage and raid your lands;
    The deluge rising, drawing near
    Shall cleanse the villages of fear.

    In this carnage One shall rise
    And lead the righteous to the skies.
And what of me? What of my life?
    You shall die this night, my Lord.

How dare you, slave, address me thus?
    'Tis not my words, and I but quote.
I shall behead you, all the same—
Are these the words of the old dolt?

    They are, my Lord, thus spoke the sage.
    If I shall perish at this stage,
Tell me how I leave this world!
    With my blade about your throat.

MY FRIENDS

My friends will never let me down;
I've got their backs and they've got mine
My friends will never let me go;
They'll fix me up, and I'll give back

My friends support me to the end
And I shall die for them some day
My friends depend on me for strength;
But I admit, I have none left.

DON'T CRY

Wipe your rainy cheeks, my friend—
Nothing lasts forever;
The darkest time of night brings forth
The brightest stars of all.

Hearts shall bleed and hearts shall heal;
The pain will scar and disappear.
When beams of light defeat the night,

The sun shall burst and burn and rise
And no more tears will fill your eyes.

CHOOSE YOUR SIDE

Your idols have abandoned you
  Betrayed your hopes and trust
    Corruption has corrupted them
    Poisoning their hearts

  Now, choose your side or die at once!
  Now choose your side, or die at once!
  Now choose your side and die, at once!

JUSTICE CAME

United nations shut their doors
The chosen few have sold the world
Justice came, but not for all
The game got rigged; some people won.

SHE DOES NOT LOVE ME ANYMORE

There is a sadness in her eyes;
She does not love me anymore.
The spark is gone—
Her eyes are cold,
Her shoulders—drooped,
Her head, like so.

And there is nothing I can do;
She does not love me anymore.

THIS TIME, I THINK

She said, "What happened?
You looked so in love."
I said we were,
    —but worlds apart.

This time,
I think I went too far;
The music stopped,
    —but I kept dancing.

A DAY AT A TIME

I kill myself—
one day at a time.

(I've broken yet another vow.)

I killed myself today—
I know . . .

(I've broken yet another heart.)

Do not fear! The pills are here!
Let's sail the skies unnerved,
the simulation must go on;
the end is nowhere to be seen.

Why is my laughter drained of joy
when I am still a child?

I killed myself, again, today,
and jerked my appetite away.

TODAY, NEXT YEAR

To our time's first Genocide
Free World Leaders close their eyes
Today, next year, they'll all be friends
In forceful fears, making amends.

I-YEARN

At first,
I left this piece untitled—
I didn't know what else to say.

Then I remembered *everything*:

Mr. ----'s sporadic beatings,
disguised as discipline.
It's discipline,
he used to say
(I guess I should be grateful).

My broken teachers—
preaching life.

The time she blew my mind:
It's pronounced I-yearn, not I-ron.

That other time she broke my heart—
when slowly I broke hers.

And then I thought of all that's good—
I'll save it for another time.

OVERTHROWN

The rebel showing off his scars
Demands the tyrant's flight
The people clashing for their lives
Put up a worthy fight

Martyrs rise up from their tombs
And return back home
The despot walking to his doom
Is being overthrown.

THEIR GLISTENING FACES

The heat—unbearable but missed
Provokes a change of hearts in all
And though at first they couldn't see
We celebrated fervidly.

Can this be it?
Can this be true?

My heart fills to the brink, again
But I don't let it spill.

And they dance
And dance
And dance.

For the first time I can see it!
For the first time I believe!

And I feel the air—so clean
And I see a new sun rising.

And their glistening faces of hope
Their glistening faces of hope.

TRAVESTY

The Parliament is being tried
For moral travesty
The whipping boys, sentenced to die
Must save His Majesty.

ONE MILLION CROSSES

I passed a cemetery today:
One million crosses in a row
One million memories to mourn
One million epitaphs in stone
I saw a mother and her child
Sit on the perfectly cut grass
The child was singing for her dad
Among the million crosses.

WITH EVERY PASSING DEATH

With every passing death, I age;
I fade with every passing death.

"There's too much pity in your heart,"
That's what she said before she left;
"And it will kill you in the end"
(Perhaps I should've left instead).

At times I cannot take it straight;
A long lost mind, asking for change
I stop and search within myself,
I give my all but come up short.

ACID RAIN

Apple seeds within my brain
Ripen in the acid rain
Someone looks and sees me through
Commanding me what I should do

Too many wires around my neck
Unwanted signals in my head
The lights are flashing day and night
I haven't slept in years

I'm still waiting for a sign
Why don't you like me anymore?
What if I fabricate a smile?
Would you still see through my disguise?

What if I told you I'm unhappy
And every day is getting worse?
Would I believe you if you told me
That filters can't disguise my woes?

What if I said that I feel hopeless?
Would you believe me if I lied?
Would I believe it if you told me
That they have seen through you
And cried?

MY EPIC

I traveled far to reach this place
The trunkless legs were gone

I'm not a native of these parts
But then again, aren't they killed?

The air is filled with wasted breath
And breathless do I feel of late

Nature stopped harvesting lives
Now all women are displeased

Perhaps I'll drink myself to death
No way, José, the cupboard's bare

Should I rise and save the world
I'd rather jerk myself to sleep

I looked up past the pollution
But the stars did not align

Progress radiates all through
In time everyone will die

I have seen and yet not seen
The fuck do I know, anyway?

We did not like the cards they dealt
So we got good at cheating

Something's surely happening
I just don't know what

Which way is right; is it the right?
The cartographers were wrong

Where can I go and not be seen?
I swear I've seen your face before

That was after it went black
And we were left all by ourselves

Lonely living leads to lusting
Too much lust diminishes

Who are you to teach me love
When all your love's been swiped

I've been drinking two weeks straight
I say it is against the cold

When I get drunk
I'll tell you how I miss you

When you get drunk
You'll say it was my fault.

THE ROAD

I can't go on; I must give in
The road's too long and filled with pain
I cannot see the finish line
Nor can I force my feet to bear
Darkness falls; all hope grows dim
And I lose heart and weep.

THE ROAD (II)

I must go on; I can't give in
No roads shall run forever!
Through my fears and meager sleep
I must persist and persevere
I must keep on for all the pain
I have endured along the way

So when the end is drawing nigh
I might stand worthy of its time.

DON'T TAKE YOUR TALENTS TO YOUR GRAVE

Don't take your talents to your grave
Don't drown your inner voice in noise
Don't let your family, friend, or foe
Dishearten you from wanting more

When time has wiped your chips away
And no more hands are left to play
Regret will plague your dreams at night
And tyrannize your tortured mind

Life will wink and pass you by
And flood the corners of your eyes
When on your deathbed, frail and gray
In fear and trembling, you shall lay.

Fortune smiles upon the brave
Don't take your talents to your grave!

THE END

Dear friend, you have reached the end of *Black Book of Poems: Part II*. Thank you for reading my work. I sincerely hope you enjoyed it!

As a last thing, would you please leave an honest review online? It is the kindness of readers like yourself that made *Black Book of Poems* into what it is today.

If you enjoyed this collection, add me on Instagram for more poetry and DM me your thoughts regarding the work.

My Instagram is: @vincenthunanyan

I am always very happy and humbled to hear from you, and I love answering your questions!

All replies come from me personally.

Thank you, and keep smiling!

ABOUT THE AUTHOR

Vincent K. Hunanyan was born in 1991 in Armenia and grew up in St. Petersburg, Russia, and later Sweden, raised by his single mother.

His self-published debut, *Black Book of Poems*, was released on May 21, 2017, and as of May 28, 2020, it has been an online bestseller for three consecutive years.

Hunanyan has also published a short story collection entitled *I Wasn't Crying Over You*, mainly based on the author's childhood and transition into adulthood.

Hunanyan's passion for writing began at the age of thirteen, when the author, together with a friend, worked on rap lyrics recorded at home and released online. In time, those lyrics became poetry.

Though Hunanyan graduated UCLA in 2015, it wasn't until two years later that he would release his debut, accepting a sales job in the interim before resigning at the end of 2016 to focus on his writing.

The title for *Black Book of Poems* comes from the song "Nobody Home" by Pink Floyd.

Hunanyan is currently working on his full-length novel.

BLACK BOOK OF POEMS: PART II
copyright © 2020 by Vincent K. Hunanyan. All rights reserved.
Printed in the United States of America. No part of this book may be
used or reproduced in any manner whatsoever without written
permission except in the case of reprints in the context of reviews.

Andrews McMeel Publishing
a division of Andrews McMeel Universal
1130 Walnut Street, Kansas City, Missouri 64106

www.andrewsmcmeel.com

www.vincenthunanyan.com
@vincenthunanyan

20 21 22 23 24 BVG 10 9 8 7 6 5 4 3 2 1

ISBN: 978-1-5248-5584-0

Library of Congress Control Number: 2019954460

Editor: Patty Rice
Art Director: Holly Swayne
Production Editor: Amy Strassner
Production Manager: Carol Coe

This book is a work of fiction. Names, characters, places, and incidents
either are products of the author's imagination or are used fictitiously.
Any resemblance to actual events or locations or persons,
living or dead, is entirely coincidental.

ATTENTION: SCHOOLS AND BUSINESSES
Andrews McMeel books are available at quantity discounts with bulk
purchase for educational, business, or sales promotional use. For information,
please e-mail the Andrews McMeel Publishing Special Sales Department:
specialsales@amuniversal.com.